PENTHOS & PASSION

PENTHOS & PASSION

SEVEN DAYS OF SPIRITUAL RENEWAL

———

Michael K. Courey

St. George Press, Los Angeles
2024

To My Beloved Wife Maria

TABLE OF CONTENTS

ACKNOWLEDGEMENTS

This book is dedicated to my beloved wife, Presbytera Maria Eleni Courey, who was my inspiration to follow my calling to the holy priesthood in the Greek Orthodox Church and to the pursuit of my visual art. Without her love and support, neither my ministry nor my art would have been possible. Our life in Christ has been a journey of faith and prayer that has been blessed with children, grandchildren, godchildren, and beloved parishioners in every church that we have had the honor to serve. Above all, I would like to thank, my Lord, God, and Savior Jesus Christ, and His life saving passion and glorious Resurrection for the salvation of the world. Much appreciation is due to my dedicated professors at Holy Cross Greek Orthodox School of Theology and Fuller Theological Seminary, whose spiritual guidance has been a major blessing in my life. Special thanks to Miss Fotini White, who took on the task of typesetting my handwritten manuscript, working many hours with persistence and perseverance. Finally, I would like to express my sincere appreciation and heartfelt gratitude to Mr. Grig Gheorghiu, for his willingness to publish my book.

LIST OF ILLUSTRATIONS

NOTE ON QUOTATIONS FROM HOLY SCRIPTURE

All quotations from the Holy Scriptures in this book are taken from *the New King James Bible, New Testament and Psalms,* Copyright 1980 by Thomas Nelson, Inc.

INTRODUCTION

When I was studying Christian Spirituality at Fuller Theological Seminary, my professor, Rev. Dr. Tom Schwanda, made a comment that led to me to return to one of my earliest artistic expressions. He said that many students had asked him over his many years of teaching to recommend a "spiritual book." His first response was always, "How about the Psalms?" In the Eastern Orthodox tradition, the Psalms remain the primary prayer book for the Church. In my reading of the Psalms, especially as a visual artist seeking inspiration from the Holy Scriptures, I was struck upon meditating on Psalm 27:7-9.

> *Hear, O Lord, when I cry with my voice!*
> *Have mercy also upon me, and answer me.*
> *When you said, "Seek My face,"*
> *My heart said to You, "Your face, Lord, I will seek."*
> *Do not hide Your face from me;*
> *Do not turn Your servant away in anger;*
> *You have been my help;*
> *Do not leave me nor forsake me,*
> *O God of my salvation.*

After meditating on this Psalm, I sought the face of the Lord by returning to my earliest artistic expression, drawing. It was the season of Great Lent and Holy Week, a season of repentance and reflection on the passion of our Lord, God, and Savior Jesus Christ. The illustrations in this book are based on my search for the face of Jesus inspired by meditations on the Holy Scripture pertaining to Holy Week in the Eastern Orthodox tradition. Furthermore, the visual journey of the act of drawing led my soul to *penthos.* Penthos, a word rooted in ancient Greek, refers to a spirit of contrition, compunction, repentance, remorse, and grief for sin. Often accompanied by what is known as *the gift of tears,* one grieves in the spirit of a *joy-creating-*

sorrow, opening a path for returning to God. Jesus taught this aspect of spirituality in His Sermon on the Mount, declaring.

"Blessed *are* those who mourn (*penthountes*),

For they shall be comforted." (Matthew 5:4)

Eastern Orthodox Christians have found comfort in the reading of the Psalms, meditation on the New Testament message of Christ's redeeming passion and glorious resurrection during the seven days of Holy Week, and the contemplative spiritual exercise of the recitation of the Jesus Prayer. The meditations in this book are selections from the New Testament that relate to the themes of *penthos* regarding the ministry, suffering, redeeming sacrificial death, and resurrection of Jesus Christ. They conclude with the expectation of Christ's return in glory for the final judgment, ushering in His eternal kingdom and the life of the age to come.

Following each meditation on the New Testament passages the reader moves to contemplative prayers of repentance in the spirit of *penthos.* The meditations on Holy Scripture and contemplative prayers are designed to be offered by the reader each morning and evening beginning on a Monday for seven consecutive days of spiritual renewal, ending on a Sunday. They may be read on any week of the calendar year. This handbook is best suited for a week set aside for a spiritual retreat. Deeply personal in nature, these contemplations are synthesis of the following Eastern Orthodox traditions: reflection on a passage from the Psalms; the Holy Week experience of seven days of worship of Jesus Christ's ministry, passion, and resurrection; and the recitation of the Jesus prayer.

Expanding the longer form of the Jesus prayer from the familiar version made popular from the classic book of Russian Orthodox spirituality, *The Way of Pilgrim,* (Lord Jesus Christ, Son of God, have mercy on me, a sinner), I have inserted my own heartfelt expressions of *penthos.* I hope that in sharing my journey upon entering the spiritual path of *katharsis* (purification of the soul through repentance), the reader will join me in an effort to develop a deeper personal relationship with our Lord, God, and Savior Jesus Christ. These meditations and contemplations are meant to be offered in solitude, stillness, and silent prayer every morning and evening for one week, for seven days of spiritual renewal through obedience to the first teaching offered in the ministry of Jesus Christ, "Repent, for the kingdom of heaven is at hand." (Matthew 4:17)

MORNING AND EVENING

MEDITATIONS ON THE INCARNATION
AND THE
PASSION OF JESUS CHRIST
WITH
CONTEMPLATIVE PRAYERS OF CONTRITION

MONDAY MORNING

Christ Sinai

Meditation: The Mystery of God Incarnate

John 1:1-17

In the beginning was the Word, and the Word was with God, and the Word was God. He was in the beginning with God. All things were made through Him, and without Him nothing was made that was made. In Him was life, and the life was the light of men. And the light shines in the darkness, and the darkness did not comprehend it. There was a man sent from God, whose name was John. This man came for a witness, to bear witness of the Light, that all through him might believe. He was not that Light, but was sent to bear witness of that Light. That was the true Light which gives light to every man coming into the world. He was in the world, and the world was made through Him, and the world did not know Him. He came to His own, and His own did not receive Him. But as many as received Him, to them He gave the right to become children of God, to those who believe in His name: who were born, not of blood, nor of the will of the flesh, nor of the will of man, but of God. And the Word became flesh and dwelt among us, and we beheld His glory, the glory as of the only begotten of the Father, full of grace and truth. John bore witness of Him and cried out saying, "This was He of whom I said, 'He who comes after me is preferred before me, for He was before me.'" And of His fullness we have all received, and grace for grace. For the law was given through Moses, but grace and truth came through Jesus Christ.

Monday Morning Contemplation

+ O Lord Jesus Christ, Son of God, eternal with God the Father and the Holy Spirit; All Holy Trinity, Creator, Giver of Life, have mercy on me, a sinner.

+ O Lord Jesus Christ, Son of God, the Light of the World, enlighten the darkness of my heart and soul; have mercy on me, a sinner.

+ O Lord Jesus Christ, Son of God, may I have the courage to bear witness of Your Light, as did John the Baptist, for although he was born in the flesh before Your birth, You were before him as the eternal Word of God before the creation of the world. O Eternal Logos have mercy on me, a sinner.

+ O Lord Jesus Christ, Son of God, the world did not know You; Your own people did not receive You; yet I desire to know You as true God, and I receive You in my mind and my heart as my Lord and Savior. I believe in Your name, receive me as a child of God, and have mercy on me, a sinner.

+ O Lord Jesus Christ, Son of God, may I be born from above, not of flesh and blood as in my bodily birth, according to human will, but may I be born of God in You and through You that I may behold Your glory; yet aware of my unworthiness, I cry out to You, have mercy on me, a sinner.

+ O Lord Jesus Christ, Son of God, You are the embodiment of the glory of the only begotten of the Father, full of grace and truth. Grant that I may receive Your grace and abide in Your truth forever. Wherefore I cry out to You, have mercy on me, a sinner.

+ O Lord Jesus Christ, Son of God, I have received from Your fullness grace for grace, truth for truth, light for light, glory for glory. For I cannot be saved by the law of Moses alone because of my transgressions, yet through Your grace and truth I have been given the right to become a child of God. Therefore, with faith and hope, I cry out to You, have mercy on me, a sinner.

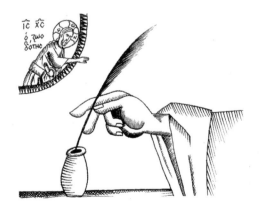

MONDAY EVENING

Christ The Merciful
Meditation: The Mystery of Christ's Mercy
John 8:1-11

Jesus went to the Mount of Olives. Now early in the morning He came again into the temple, and all the people came to Him; and He sat down and taught them. Then the scribes and Pharisees brought to Him a woman caught in adultery. And when they had set her in the midst, they said to Him, "Teacher, this woman was caught in adultery, in the very act. Now Moses, in the law, commanded us that such should be stoned. But what do You say?" This they said, testing Him, that they might have something of which to accuse Him. But Jesus stooped down and wrote on the ground with His finger, as though He did not hear. So when they continued asking Him, He raised Himself up and said to them, "He who is without sin among you, let him throw a stone at her first." And again He stooped down and wrote on the ground. Then those who heard it, being convicted by their conscience, went out one by one, beginning with the oldest even to the last. And Jesus was left alone, and the woman standing in the midst. When Jesus had raised Himself up and saw no one but the woman, He said to her, "Woman, where are those accusers of yours? Has no one condemned you?" She said, "No one, Lord." And Jesus said to her, "Neither do I condemn you; go and sin no more."

Monday Evening Contemplation

+ O Lord Jesus Christ, Son of God, teach me how to live by Your words, Your actions, Your love, Your gentleness, Your compassion, and have mercy on me, a sinner.

+ O Lord Jesus Christ, Son of God, forbid me to behave as the scribes and Pharisees, putting You to the test. Seeking to accuse You while accusing others. In doing such I accuse myself, for I am the chief among sinners. Therefore, I beg of You, have mercy on me, a sinner.

+ O Lord Jesus Christ, Son of God, like the woman caught in the very act of adultery, I have been set before You in the midst of my accusers. I am guilty of sin and my sentence, according to the law, should be death. I will face Your judgement throne and the demons will accuse me of my iniquities. Therefore, I cry out to You, have mercy on me, a sinner.

+ O Lord Jesus Christ, Son of God, You wrote on the ground in silence before those who accused the woman of her sin. Do not, I beg You, keep a written record of my sins. O my Savior, by Your precious blood shed on the cross for my salvation, I beseech You, blot out my transgressions and have mercy on me, a sinner.

+ O Lord Jesus Christ, Son of God, as the accusers, convicted by their conscience, left the woman they accused of adultery one by one, so may I be convicted of my sin and never throw a stone of judgement or condemnation at anyone again. O Merciful One, full of compassion, have mercy on me, a sinner.

+ O Lord Jesus Christ, Son of God, like the woman caught in adultery, I will stand alone in fear and trembling before Your judgement throne, because of my sins. Yet I dare to plea Your precious blood over the multitude of my transgressions, and I beg of You, O righteous Judge, to have mercy on me, a sinner.

+ O Lord Jesus Christ, Son of God, disperse the demons who accuse me of my sins before Your righteous Judgement throne. By Your precious blood, I plea, may those who seek my condemnation depart from me, although I am guilty as accused. For I am truly sorry for my sins, and I resolve to go and sin no more. As you did not condemn the adulterous woman, I beg of You, O merciful Lord, do not condemn me, and have mercy on me, a sinner.

TUESDAY MORNING

Christ Transfigured
Meditation: The Mystery of the Uncreated Light
Matthew 17:1-3; Luke 9:32,33; Matthew 17: 5-9

Now...Jesus took Peter, James and John his brother, led them up a high mountain by themselves; and He was transfigured before them. His face shone like the sun, and His clothes became as white as the light. As He prayed, the appearance of His face was altered, and His robe became white and glistening. And behold, Moses and Elijah appeared to them, talking with Him. But Peter and those with him were heavy with sleep; and when they were fully awake, they saw His glory and the two men who stood with Him. Then it happened, as they were parting from Him, that Peter said to Jesus, "Master, it is good for us to be here; and let us make three tabernacles: one for You, one for Moses, and one for Elijah" - not knowing what he said. While he was still speaking, behold, a bright cloud overshadowed them; and suddenly a voice came out of the cloud, saying, "This is My beloved Son, in whom I am well pleased. Hear Him!" And when the disciples heard it, they fell on their faces and were greatly afraid. But Jesus came and touched them and said, "Arise, and do not be afraid." When they had lifted up their eyes, they saw no one but Jesus only. Now as they came down from the mountain, Jesus commanded them, saying, "Tell the vision to no one until the Son of Man is risen from the dead."

Tuesday Morning Contemplation

+ O Lord Jesus Christ, Son of God, please take me to the high mountain to pray with You, as You took Peter, James and John. Yet I am aware of my unworthiness to be in Your company with Your disciples. Therefore, I cry out to you, have mercy on me a sinner.

+ O Lord Jesus Christ, Son of God, You were transfigured before Peter, James, and John and Your holy face shone like the sun. Your clothing became as white as Your uncreated light that shined forth from Your all-pure body. O Lord, purify my face, my body, and even my clothing by the bright light of Your countenance and have mercy on me, a sinner.

+ O Lord Jesus Christ, Son of God, like Peter, James and John, You took me to pray with You. But I, heavy in the sleep of my sin, am not fully aware of Your divinity. Wake me fully from my slumber to pray that I may converse with You as did Moses and Elijah, in this life and in the life to come. For the work that You accomplished in Jerusalem was Your life-saving death on the cross. Save me, O Transfigured One, from the heavy darkness of my passions, and have mercy on me, a sinner.

+ O Lord Jesus Christ, Son of God, like Peter, beholding You with Moses and Elijah, I see the law and the prophecy fulfilled in Your glory. Yet I cannot, though I desire as Peter did, contain You and Your saints in an earthly dwelling place like the tabernacle of old. Wherefore I cry out to You, not knowing what I am saying, O Lord, I desire to be in a good place of prayer with You and the Saints here and now, and for ever and ever. O Transfigured One, Light of Light, true God of true God, I long for my heart to be a dwelling place for Your Holy Spirit, and so I cry out to You, have mercy on me a sinner.

+ O Lord Jesus Christ, Son of God, overshadow me with the bright cloud of Your Holy Spirit, and have mercy on me, a sinner.

+ O Lord Jesus Christ, Son of God, let me hear You as God the Father spoke to Your disciples saying, "This is My beloved Son, in whom I am well pleased, hear Him!" May my prayer be pleasing to You, O my Savior, and have mercy on me, a sinner.

+ O Lord Jesus Christ, Son of God, I fall on my face to the ground in fear, in awe, in faith, and in love for You, O my God. Touch me as You touched Peter, James, and John. Raise me up from the earth and lift up my eyes to behold Your face which I seek, O Lord. Give me Your grace, the courage, and the wisdom to tell others of Your glorious Transfiguration and Resurrection from the dead, and have mercy on me, a sinner.

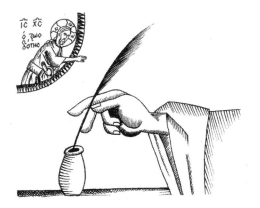

TUESDAY EVENING

Christ the Light-giver
Meditation: The Mystery of the Uncreated Light
John 8:12; 12:35,36; Matthew 5:14-16

Then Jesus spoke to them (the Pharisees) again, saying, "I am the light of the world. He who follows Me shall not walk in darkness, but have the light of life."

"Walk while you have the light, lest darkness overtake you; he who walks in darkness does not know where he is going. While you have the light, believe in the light, that you may become sons of light.

"You are the light of the world. A city that is set on a hill cannot be hidden. Nor do they light a lamp and put it under a basket, but on a lampstand, and it gives light to all who are in the house. Let your light so shine before men, that they may see your good works and glorify your Father in heaven."

Tuesday Evening Contemplation

+ O Lord Jesus Christ, Son of God, You are the Light that is never overtaken by night; have mercy on me, a sinner.

+ O Lord Jesus Christ, Son of God, enlighten my path that I may walk in Your light; have mercy on me, a sinner.

+ O Lord Jesus Christ, Son of God, let not the darkness overtake my soul, lest I be led astray by the prince of darkness; have mercy on me, a sinner.

+ O Lord Jesus Christ, Son of God, I believe in You and in Your Light, have mercy on me, a sinner.

+ O Lord Jesus Christ, Son of God, guide me in Your light, that I may become a child of light; have mercy on me, a sinner.

+ O Lord Jesus Christ, Son of God, illumine my mind that I may be light as You are the Light; have mercy on me, a sinner.

+ O Lord Jesus Christ, Son of God, shine Your Light on me that the work of my life may be light before men to the glory of God the Father. Amen.

WEDNESDAY MORNING

Man of Sorrows
Meditation: The Mystery of Christ's Extreme Humility
Isaiah 53:2-5

He has no form or comeliness; and when we see Him, there is no beauty that we should desire Him. He is despised and rejected by men, a Man of sorrows and acquainted with grief. And we hid, as it were, our faces from Him; He was despised, and we did not esteem Him. Surely He has borne our griefs and carried our sorrows; yet we esteemed Him stricken, smitten by God, and afflicted. But He was wounded for our transgressions, He was bruised for our iniquities; the chastisement for our peace was upon Him, and by His stripes we are healed.

Wednesday Morning Contemplation

+ O Lord Jesus Christ, Son of God, in Your passion You received the buffeting, the beating, the scourging, so that Your beauty and majesty was disfigured because of my sins; have mercy on me, a sinner.

+ O Lord Jesus Christ, Son of God, my sin has caused Your sorrow and suffering, forgive me for despising and rejecting You; have mercy on me, a sinner.

+ O Lord Jesus Christ, Son of God, forgive me for hiding my face from You; have mercy on me, a sinner.

+ O Lord Jesus Christ, Son of God, I recognize and acknowledge that You took up my infirmity and carried my sorrows with Your suffering; have mercy on me, a sinner.

+ O Lord Jesus Christ, Son of God, forgive me for not holding You in esteem; have mercy on me, a sinner.

+ O Lord Jesus Christ, Son of God, You were stricken by God the Father for my sins, forgive me for afflicting You; have mercy on me, a sinner.

+ O Lord Jesus Christ, Son of God, I pierced Your hands, Your feet, Your forehead, and Your side because of my sin, and You were crushed because of my iniquity. Forgive me, heal me, save me, and have mercy on me, a sinner.

WEDNESDAY EVENING

Agony in the Garden
Meditation: The Mystery of the Human and Divine Wills
Luke 22:39-46

Jesus went to the Mount of Olives, as He was accustomed, and His disciples also followed Him. When He came to the place, He said to them, "Pray that you may not enter into temptation." And He was withdrawn from them about a stone's throw, and He knelt down and prayed, saying, "Father, if it is Your will, take this cup away from Me; nevertheless not My will, but Yours, be done."

Then an angel appeared to Him from heaven, strengthening Him. And being in agony, He prayed more earnestly. Then His sweat became like great drops of blood falling down to the ground. When He rose up from prayer, and had come to His disciples, He found them sleeping from sorrow. Then He said to them, "Why do you sleep? Rise and pray, lest you enter into temptation."

Wednesday Evening Contemplation

+ O Lord Jesus Christ, Son of God, teach me to pray as You prayed, and have mercy on me, a sinner.

+ O Lord Jesus Christ, Son of God, guide me to a private place to pray, and have mercy on me, a sinner.

+ O Lord Jesus Christ, Son of God, hear me as I kneel before Your Father and my Father, and have mercy on me, a sinner.

+ O Lord Jesus Christ, Son of God, show me how to surrender to the will of the Father, and have mercy on me, a sinner.

+ O Lord Jesus Christ, Son of God, in the face of temptations send me an angel to give me strength, and have mercy on me, a sinner.

+ O Lord Jesus Christ, Son of God, grant me the gift of tears of repentance that my tears may fall from my face to the ground. O You who suffered in the agony of the garden of Gethsemane for my salvation, have mercy on me, a sinner.

+ O Lord Jesus Christ, Son of God, You found me sleeping from the sorrow of my sins. Raise me to pray, that I may not enter into temptation, and have mercy on me, a sinner.

THURSDAY MORNING

Christ Betrayed

Meditation: The Mystery of the Sorrowful Passion
Mt 17:22,23; Mt 26:14-16, 36-50; Lk 22:48

Jesus said to them, "The Son of Man is about to be betrayed into the hands of men, and they will kill Him, and the third day He will be raised up." And they were exceedingly sorrowful. Then one of the twelve, called Judas Iscariot, went to the chief priests and said, "What are you willing to give me, if I deliver Him to you?" And they counted out to him thirty pieces of silver. So from that time he sought the opportunity to betray Him. Jesus came...to a place called Gethsemane, and said to the disciples, "Sit here while I go and pray over there." And He took with Him Peter and the two sons of Zebedee, and He began to be sorrowful and deeply distressed. Then He said to them, "My soul is exceedingly sorrowful, even to death. Stay here and watch with me." He went a little farther and fell on His face, and prayed, saying, "O My Father, if it is possible, let this cup pass from Me; nevertheless, not as I will, but as you will. The He came to the disciples and found them sleeping, and said to Peter, "What? Could you not watch with me one hour? Watch and pray, lest you enter into temptation. The spirit indeed is willing, but the flesh is weak. Again, a second time He prayed, saying, "O My Father, if this cup cannot pass away from me unless I drink it, Your will be done." And He came and found them asleep again, and prayed the third time, saying the same words. Then He came to His disciples and said to them, "Are you still sleeping and resting? Behold, the hour is at hand, and the Son of Man is being betrayed into the hands of sinners. Rise, let us be going. See, my betrayer is at hand. And while He was still speaking, behold, Judas, one of the twelve, with a great multitude with swords and clubs, came from the chief priests and elders of the people. Now His betrayer had given them a sign, saying, "Whomever I kiss, He is the one; seize Him." Immediately he went up to Jesus and said, "Greetings, Rabbi!" and kissed Him.

But Jesus said to him, "Friend, why have you come? Judas, are you betraying the Son of Man with a kiss?"

Thursday Morning Contemplation

+ O Lord Jesus Christ, Son of God, I sorrow with exceedingly great grief that I have betrayed you with my sinfulness, I beg of You on account of Your third day resurrection from the dead to have mercy on me, a sinner.

+ O Lord Jesus Christ, Son of God, like Your disciples I have fallen asleep and rested instead of keeping watch and praying with You. I beg You to forgive my slothfulness and have mercy on me, a sinner.

+ O Lord Jesus Christ, Son of God, the hour is at hand. Grant that I may I rise up with You in prayer, rather than betray You in the face of my sinfulness. Wherefore I cry out to You, have mercy on me, a sinner.

+ O Lord Jesus Christ, Son of God, with the chief priests and the elders, and the multitude with swords and clubs, I led the crowd like Judas to betray You, my Savior. Wherefore I cry out to You to forgive me and have mercy on me, a sinner.

+ O Lord Jesus Christ, Son of God, I called You Rabbi and teacher as did Judas, one of Your twelve chosen. Yet I gave a sign to Satan, and I betrayed You with a kiss on Your most holy face as did Judas. Now in full repentance I bow down to kiss Your sacred feet, pierced with nails for my sins, and I beg You to have mercy on me, a sinner.

+ O Lord Jesus Christ, Son of God, have I come to You who calls me friend as You called Your betrayer Judas? Have I come to betray You with a kiss? Have I come to greet You falsely? Have I come to You in the blindness of my pride and foolishness of my sin? But now, O Lord, I come to You on bended knees with upraised arms and bowed head, begging You to forgive me for my transgressions and to have mercy on me, a sinner.

+ O Lord Jesus Christ, Son of God, am I betraying You with a kiss as did Judas? Am I approaching You with ill intent and in ignorance of Your divinity? Am I guilty of betraying Your righteousness? I am a sinner, and the first of sinners, but I resolve not to betray You from this day forth with a kiss as did Judas - but like the repentant thief I confess You - remember me, O Lord, in Your kingdom and have mercy on me, a sinner.

THURSDAY EVENING

Christ Scourged
Meditation: The Sorrowful Mystery of Christ's
Innocent Suffering
Mt. 27:24; I Peter 2:21-24

When Pilate saw that he could not prevail at all... he took water and washed his hands before the multitude saying, "I am innocent of the blood of this just person"... and when he had scourged Jesus, he delivered Him to be crucified.

For to this you were called, because Christ also suffered for us, leaving us an example, that you should follow His steps:
"Who committed no sin,
Nor was deceit found in His mouth";
who, when He was reviled, did not revile in return; when He suffered, He did not threaten, but committed Himself to Him who judges righteously; who Himself bore our sins in His own body on the tree, that we, having died to sins, might live for righteousness - by whose stripes you were healed.

Thursday Evening Contemplation

+ O Lord Jesus Christ, Son of God, I am not innocent of Your precious blood shed for my sins; have mercy on me, a sinner.

+ O Lord Jesus Christ, Son of God, You suffered for my sins, You were innocent and suffered for my salvation; have mercy on me, a sinner.

+ O Lord Jesus Christ, Son of God, may I follow Your example and sin no more, nor may there be found any more deceit in my mouth; O You who are without sin; have mercy on me, a sinner.

+ O Lord Jesus Christ, Son of God, teach me to be like You when I am reviled, that I may not revile in return; and have mercy on me, a sinner.

+ O Lord Jesus Christ, Son of God, when I experience suffering, show me how to be like You, and not to threaten others; and have mercy on me, a sinner.

+ O Lord Jesus Christ, Son of God, You who bore my sins on Your body and died on the cross, may I also die to my sins. Have mercy on me, a sinner.

+ O Lord Jesus Christ, Son of God, lead me on the path of righteousness, You who heal my wounded soul, by the stripes of your scourging; have mercy on me, a sinner.

FRIDAY MORNING

Christ the Bridegroom

Meditation: The Sorrowful Mystery of Christ arrested, bound, spat upon, beaten, struck, denied, pierced with a crown of thorns, and mocked with a reed and purple robe.
John 18:12; Mt. 26:67, 69-75; Jn 19:2-5

Then the detachment of troops and the captain and the officers of the Jews arrested Jesus and bound Him.

Then they spat in His face and beat Him; and others struck Him with the palms of their hands. Now Peter sat outside in the courtyard. And a servant girl came to him saying, "You also were with Jesus of Galilee." But he denied it before them all, saying, "I do not know what you are saying. And when he had gone to the gateway, another girl saw him and said to those who were there, "This fellow also was with Jesus of Nazareth". But again he denied with an oath, "I do not know the Man!" And a little later those who stood by came up and said to Peter, "Surely you are one of them, for your speech betrays you." Then he began to curse and swear, saying, "I do not know the Man!" Immediately a rooster crowed. And Peter remembered the word of Jesus who had said to him, "Before the rooster crows, you will deny me three times," so he went out and wept bitterly.

And the soldiers twisted a crown of thorns and put it on Jesus' head, and they put on Him a purple robe. Then they said, "Hail, King of the Jews!" And they struck Him with their hands. Pilate then went out and said, "Behold, I am bringing Him out to you, that you may know that I find no fault in Him." Then Jesus came out, wearing the crown of thorns and the purple robe. And Pilate said to them, "Behold the Man!"

Friday Morning Contemplation

+ O Lord Jesus Christ, Son of God, You were arrested and bound, spat upon, beaten, and struck for my sake. You took the punishment for my transgressions. Wherefore I cry out to You, have mercy on me, a sinner.

+ O Lord Jesus Christ, Son of God, like Peter, out of fear of what others might think, say, or do if they discovered that I have followed You, I have denied that I know You. O my Savior. Have mercy on me, a sinner.

+ O Lord Jesus Christ, Son of God, like Peter my speech has betrayed my denial of You as my Lord, God, and Savior because of my fear of the crowd. But like Peter, I repent with bitter tears, and I weep and lament my denial. Have mercy on me, a sinner.

+ O Lord Jesus Christ, Son of God, You who are the true King of Kings, were mocked by the soldiers with a crown of thorns, a purple robe, and a reed. Like the soldiers I have mocked and struck You with my willful disobedience of Your law. Yet I repent and cry out like Peter. Have mercy on me, a sinner.

+ O Lord Jesus Christ, Son of God, You were brought before me as the bridegroom of the church. You loved Your church and gave Yourself to her. You sanctified the church and cleansed her by Your precious blood shed for our salvation. Have mercy on me, a sinner.

+ O Lord Jesus Christ, Son of God, the church is Your bride. The great mystery of salvation by Your sacrificial marriage brings me, though unworthy, into a mystical union with You. In awe of Your nuptial love, aware of my transgressions, I cry out to You, have mercy on me, a sinner.

+ O Lord Jesus Christ, Son of God, behold You will come again in glory to present Yourself as the King of glory to judge the living and the dead. When You return in glory at the last judgement, I beg of You, my King and my God, have mercy on me, a sinner.

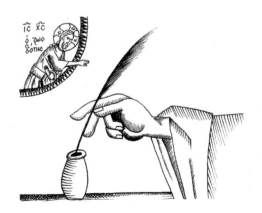

FRIDAY EVENING

Christ Carrying His Cross
Meditation: The Sorrowful Mystery of the Crucifixion
Mk 8:27, 29, 31, 34-36; Jn 19:17

Now Jesus... asked His disciples... "Who do men say that I am?" Peter answered and said to Him, "You are the Christ." And He began to teach them that the Son of Man must suffer many things and be rejected by the elders and chief priests and scribes, and be killed, and after three days rise again.

The Lord said, "Whoever desires to come after Me, let him deny himself, and take up his cross, and follow Me. For whoever desires to save his life will lose it, but whoever loses his life for My sake and the gospel's will save it. For what will it profit a man if he gains the whole world, and loses his own soul?"

And He, bearing His cross, went out to a place called the Place of a Skull, which is called in Hebrew, Golgotha, where they crucified Him, and two others with Him, one on either side, and Jesus in the center.

Friday Evening Contemplative Prayer

+ O Lord Jesus Christ, Son of God, You are the Messiah, the Anointed One, the King of Kings, the Lord of Lords, the Son of Man who suffered many things for my soul's salvation; Have mercy on me, a sinner.

+ O Lord Jesus Christ, Son of God, You are the teacher of teachers, yet the elders rejected Your teaching. You are the great high priest, but the chief priests despised You. You are the Divine Logos, the Word of God made flesh, but the scribes did not recognize You. I receive You, O Lord, and I confess You as my King and my God. Wherefore, I cry out to You, have mercy on me, a sinner.

+ O Lord Jesus Christ, Son of God, who was crucified, buried, and who rose on the third day; crucify me with You, bury me with You, raise me up from the dead with You, and have mercy on me, a sinner.

+ O Lord Jesus Christ, Son of God, I desire to come after You, but I am afraid to deny myself and to take up my cross as I am a slave to the sins of my flesh. Help me to follow You on the path of self-denial.

+ O Lord Jesus Christ, Son of God, may I crucify my evil passions and desires that war against my soul. May I die to my selfish will and do Your will alone. O You who did the will of the Father, have mercy on me, a sinner.

+ O Lord Jesus Christ, Son of God, I desire to save my own life in the selfish pursuit of the pleasures of the flesh and yet I lose my soul in my sinfulness. I desire even more, O Lord Jesus, to follow You and lose my life for Your sake and for the sake of the gospel. Help me to follow this noble desire, that my soul may live for Your sake. O Lord Jesus, save my soul and have mercy on me, a sinner.

+ O Lord Jesus Christ, Son of God, there is no profit for my soul in the acquisition of worldly goods, yet my desire for worldly gain has chained my body and soul to the world, bound in the chains and locks of greed. Break, O Lord Jesus, the bondage that binds me, set me free, and have mercy on me, a sinner.

+ O Lord Jesus Christ, Son of God, You bore the heavy weight of the sins of the world as You carried Your cross to Golgotha. The place of the skull of Adam is also the place of the death of my soul in sin. Yet through Your voluntary suffering and death my soul is set free from the tomb of Hades and the torment of eternal punishment. By the might of Your precious and life-giving cross have mercy on me, a sinner.

SATURDAY MORNING

Christ Crucified
Meditation: The Sorrowful Mystery of
Christ's Death on the Cross

Luke 23:33,34; Luke 23:42,43,46; Mt 27:45,46; John 19:25-30

And when they had come to the place called Calvary, there they crucified Him, and the criminals, one on the right and the other on the left. Then Jesus said, "Father, forgive them, for they do not know what they do." Then one of the criminals said to Jesus, "Lord, remember me when You come into Your kingdom." And Jesus said to him, "Assuredly, I say to you, today you will be with Me in Paradise." Now from the sixth hour until the ninth hour there was darkness over all the land. And about the ninth hour Jesus cried out with a loud voice, saying, "Eli, Eli, lama sabachthani?" That is, "My God, My God, why have you forsaken me?" Now there stood by the cross of Jesus His mother... when Jesus therefore saw His mother, and the disciple whom He loved standing by, He said to His mother, "Woman, behold your son!" Then He said to the disciple, "Behold your mother!" And from that hour that disciple took her to his own home. After this, Jesus, knowing that all things were now accomplished, that the Scripture might be fulfilled, said, "I thirst!" Now a vessel full of sour wine was sitting there; and they filled a sponge with sour wine, put it on hyssop, and put it to His mouth. So when Jesus had received the sour wine, He said, "It is finished!" And Jesus cried out with a loud voice, "Father, 'into Your hands I commit My spirit.'" And bowing His head, He gave up His spirit.

Saturday Morning Contemplation

+ O Lord Jesus Christ, Son of God, forgive me as You forgave those who crucified You in the flesh, for I have crucified You with my willful disobedience. Forgive me, for like those who crucified You, I know not what I do. So I beg of You, my Savior, have mercy on me, a sinner.

+ O Lord Jesus Christ, Son of God, like the thief on the cross I confess You as my King, crying out to You, "Lord, remember me when You come into Your kingdom." When the time comes for my soul to leave my body, I hope to hear You say to me, as You said to the repentant thief, "Assuredly, I say to you, today you will be with me in Paradise." Wherefore, I cry out to You, have mercy on me, a sinner.

+ O Lord Jesus Christ, Son of God, I cry out to You with a loud voice in the dark night of my soul, do not utterly forsake me, O my God, my God, and have mercy on me, a sinner.

+ O Lord Jesus Christ, Son of God, as Your disciple took Your holy mother to his own home as her son, may the door of my house of prayer be open to Your holy mother and all of Your Saints. May Your holy mother intercede for the salvation of my soul, and may You have mercy on me, a sinner.

+ O Lord Jesus Christ, Son of God, my soul thirsts for You, as the deer thirsts for the water of the brook. As You cried out on the cross, "I thirst", so I cry out to You, "I thirst, O Lord, for union with You." Therefore, my thirsty soul cries out, have mercy on me, a sinner.

+ O Lord Jesus Christ, Son of God, when Your life saving work of suffering on the cross was accomplished, You said, "It is finished". With faith in Your life-giving death for my salvation, I cry, have mercy on me, and save me.

+ O Lord Jesus Christ, Son of God, You cried out with Your last breath in a loud voice, "Father, into Your hands I commit My spirit". Bowing my head as You did when You gave up Your spirit, I bow my head to You, my Lord and my God, and I commit myself, my family, my community, and my whole life to You, my Christ. Therefore, I cry out with a loud voice, have mercy on me, a sinner.

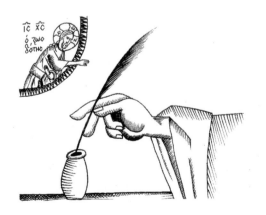

SATURDAY EVENING

Christ Reposed

Meditation: The Sorrowful Mystery of Christ in the Tomb
Mt 27:57-60; Mk 15:42-46; Luke 23:50-56; John 19:41

Now when evening had come, because it was Friday, the Preparation Day, that is the day before the Sabbath, there came a rich man from Arimathea, a prominent council member, named Joseph, who himself had also become a disciple of Jesus, but secretly for fear of the Jews. He was a good and just man, who was himself waiting for the Kingdom of God. He had not consented to the decision deed of the council. Coming and taking courage this man went to Pilate and asked for the body of Jesus. Then Pilate commanded the body to be given to him. He wrapped it in a clean linen cloth and laid it in his new tomb in which no one had yet been laid, which he had hewn out of the rock. And Nicodemus, who at first came to Jesus by night, also came, bringing a mixture of myrrh and aloes, about a hundred pounds. They took the body of Jesus, and bound it in strips of linen with the spices, as the custom of the Jews is to bring. Now in the place where He was crucified there was a garden, and in the garden the new tomb, and they rolled a large stone against the door of the tomb, and departed. And the women who had come with Him from Galilee followed after and they observed the tomb and how His body was laid. Then they returned and prepared spices and fragrant oils. And they rested on the Sabbath according to the commandment.

Saturday Evening Contemplation

+ O Lord Jesus Christ, Son of God, how I long to be Your disciple, like Joseph of Arimathea and Nicodemus. Unlike them I am neither good nor just, yet I seek you in the morning, in the evening, and in the night. Have mercy on me, a sinner, and save me.

+ O Lord Jesus Christ, Son of God, like Joseph may I also take courage to approach Your pure and sacred body, and like Nicodemus may I bring myrrh, as the wise men did at Your birth, to anoint Your precious body which suffered even unto death. O immortal One, have mercy on me, a sinner, and save me.

+ O Lord Jesus Christ, Son of God, Joseph brought clean linen to clothe Your sacred body for burial. Wrap me in clean linen, O my God, that I may put on You as a new baptismal garment. O my Jesus, as I behold Your face asleep as You lay in the tomb, I cry out to You, have mercy on me, a sinner, and save me.

+ O Lord Jesus Christ, Son of God, may I have the courage to follow You as the women who came to Your tomb with spices and fragrant oils. Observing where Your body was laid they also observed the law of Moses and rested on the Sabbath. May I also find rest in You, O my Savior, have mercy on me, a sinner, and save me.

+ O Lord Jesus Christ, Son of God, Your sacred body rested in the tomb on the Sabbath day, according to the law of Moses, the law that You came to fulfill. May I also observe the Sabbath with You and find rest for my weary body and soul in the comfort of Your loving arms, O my Savior, have mercy on me and save me.

+ O Lord Jesus Christ, Son of God, near the place where You were crucified for my soul's salvation there was a garden, and in the garden a new tomb. As Adam and Eve were driven from the garden of Eden because of their sin, so I too am forsaken from Paradise. Yet Your garden tomb renews my soul as I await Your glorious resurrection. For the stone will be rolled away and the door of the tomb shall open as You rise forth on the third day. O You who were laid in the garden tomb so that I may return to the garden of Paradise have mercy on me and save me.

+ O Lord Jesus Christ, Son of God, Your tomb where no one had lain before, like the holy womb of Your mother, the Theotokos and Ever Virgin Mary, was pure and untouched. At Your birth from the virgin womb You were wrapped in swaddling clothes and laid in a manger in a cave. After Your death on the cross You were wrapped in a burial shroud and laid in a tomb in a garden. From the womb to the tomb, the mystery of Your incarnation lies in Your condescension for humankind and for our salvation. Have mercy on me, a sinner, and save me.

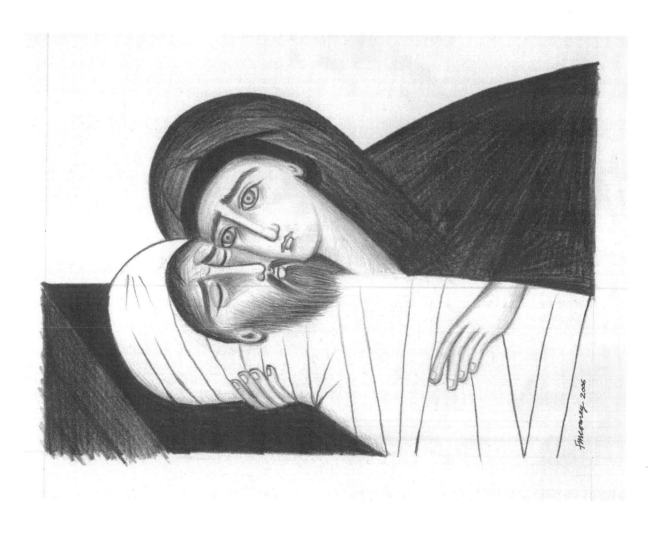

SUNDAY MORNING

Christ Resurrected

Meditation on the Christ's Glorious Resurrection from the Dead

I Cor 15:20-22; 45-47; 54-57

Christ is risen from the dead, and has become the first fruits of those who have fallen asleep. For since by man came death, by Man also came the resurrection of the dead. For as in Adam all die, even so in Christ all shall be made alive... and so it is written. "The first man Adam became a living being. The last Adam became a life-giving spirit. However, the spiritual is not first, but the natural, and afterward the spiritual. The first man was of the earth, made of dust; the second Man is the Lord from heaven... so when this corruptible has put on incorruption, and this mortal has put on immortality, then shall be brought to pass the saying that is written, "Death is swallowed up in victory."

"O Death, where is your sting?
O Hades, where is your victory?"

The sting of death is sin, and the strength of sin is the law. But thanks be to God, who gives us the victory through our Lord Jesus Christ.

Sunday Morning Contemplation

+ O Lord Jesus Christ, Son of God, You are risen from the dead… raise me up with You from the darkness of my sin into the light of Your glorious resurrection, and have mercy on me, a sinner.

+ O Lord Jesus Christ, Son of God, like Adam and Eve I have been tempted and led astray from Your law. I have chosen the death of disobedience to Your commandments, but You who have been raised from the dead - raise me with You from death to life and have mercy on me, a sinner.

+ O Lord Jesus Christ, Son of God, as You breathed life into Adam who You created from the earth… so breathe Your Holy Spirit into me. Raise my soul and body up from earth to heaven… and have mercy on me, a sinner.

+ O Lord Jesus Christ, Son of God, I am but dust and earth - from the earth I was created by You and unto the earth I shall return in body… but I pray unto You to save my soul and body from corruption to incorruption and have mercy on me, a sinner.

+ O Lord Jesus Christ, Son of God, who am I but a mere mortal to hope for immortality? Yet I long to remain in You and to be saved from the darkness of death. Have mercy; have mercy; have mercy on me, a sinner.

+ O Lord Jesus Christ, Son of God, You trampled upon death by Your death and swallowed up Hades in victory. You conquered death and removed the sting of Hades by Your Holy Resurrection. Save me from eternal punishment, and have mercy on me, a sinner.

+ O Lord Jesus Christ, Son of God, I have tried to obey Your law from my youth, but many passions have overwhelmed me. I have fallen into the deep, dark pit of sin. Save me from this abyss and raise me up by the power of Your mighty outstretched arm, full of strength and victory, and have mercy on me, a sinner.

SUNDAY EVENING

Christic the Almighty
Rev 1:8,11,17,18; 2:5,7
2:10,11,17,26,28; 3:5,12,19,20,21; 22:16,20

"I am the Alpha and the Omega, the Beginning and the End," says the Lord, "who is and who was and who is to come, the Almighty. I am the Alpha and the Omega, the First and the Last. Do not be afraid... I am He who lives, and was dead, and behold, I am alive forevermore. Amen. And I have the keys of Hades and Death. Remember therefore from where you have fallen; repent. He who has an ear, let him hear what the Spirit says to the churches. To him who overcomes I will give to eat from the tree of life, which is in the midst of the Paradise of God. Do not fear any of those things which you are about to suffer... that you may be tested... Be faithful until death, and I will give you the crown of life. He who overcomes shall not be hurt by the second death. To him who overcomes I will give some of the hidden manna to eat; ...I will give power over the nations; I will give him the morning star; He who overcomes shall be clothed in white garments, and I will not blot out his name from the Book of Life; but I will confess his name before My Father and before His angels; I will make him a pillar in the temple of My God; I will write on him the name of My God and the name of the city of My God, the New Jerusalem which comes down out of heaven. And I will write on him My new name. As many as I love, I rebuke and chasten. Therefore be zealous and repent. Behold, I stand at the door and knock. If anyone hears My voice and opens the door, I will come in to him and dine with him and he with me. To him who overcomes I will grant to sit with Me on My throne, as I also overcame and sat down with My Father on His throne. I, Jesus, have sent My angel to testify to you these things in the churches. I am the Root and the offspring of David, the Bright and Morning Star. Surely, I am coming quickly."

Amen. Even so, come, Lord Jesus!

Sunday Evening Contemplation

+ O Lord Jesus Christ, Son of God, I am afraid of Your majesty because of my unworthiness. O You who was, and is, and who is to come, the Almighty. You who hold the keys of Hades and Death; the Alpha and the Omega, the beginning and the end, the first and the last, have mercy on me, a sinner.

+ O Lord Jesus Christ, Son of God, I recall that I have fallen from grace, wherefore I repent. I hear what the Spirit says to the church, and so I cry out in the spirit of repentance, have mercy on me, a sinner.

+ O Lord Jesus Christ, Son of God, I hunger to eat from the tree of life, I who am dead in sinfulness. I long to be with You in the midst of Your Paradise, wherefore I cry out, have mercy on me, a sinner.

+ O Lord Jesus Christ, Son of God, I am fearful of suffering and being tested. Grant me strength and courage to overcome the temptations of the devil. May I finish the race and receive the crown of life - not to be hurt by the second death of eternal punishment in Hades. So that I may be fed with heavenly food in Paradise I beg You to have mercy on me, a sinner.

+ O Lord Jesus Christ, Son of God, grant me power to overcome those that war against my soul. May the light of Your morning star shine upon me that I may be clothed with pure white garments with the saints at Your heavenly altar. Do not blot out my name from Your Book of Life - rather confess my name before Your Father and His angels. My King and my Lord, make me a pillar in the heavenly temple of Your God and my God. With desire to dwell with You in Your kingdom forever, I cry out, have mercy on me, a sinner.

+ O Lord Jesus Christ, Son of God, write Your name on me. Make me a citizen of the city of God, the New Jerusalem, the heavenly city. Write on me a new name - Your new name. Renew me in Your love. Rebuke and chasten me, that I may be zealous for Your kingdom and repent of my sins. O You who stand at the door of my heart and knock - behold, I hear Your voice and open the door to You. Come into me, dine with me, and dwell in me. So that I may be found worthy to sit with You and Your Father, I beg You, have mercy on me, a sinner.

+ O Lord Jesus Christ, Son of God, send me an angel of courage, of power, of might, of strength, that I may testify and witness of Your saving grace to the churches. O Root and offspring of King David, Bright Morning Star of glory, King of Kings and Lord of Lords, who shall come in glory to judge the living and the dead, I look for the Resurrection of the dead and the life of the world to come. Come quickly, O Lord Jesus, come and save me and have mercy on me, a sinner. Amen. Even so, come, Lord Jesus!